THIS BOOK BELONG
TO 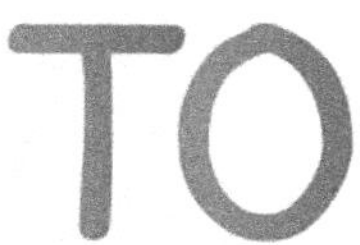......................................

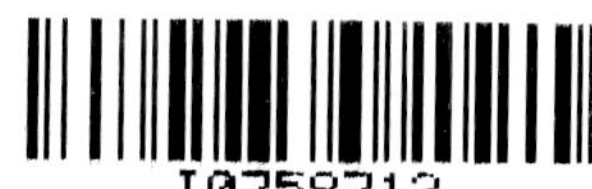

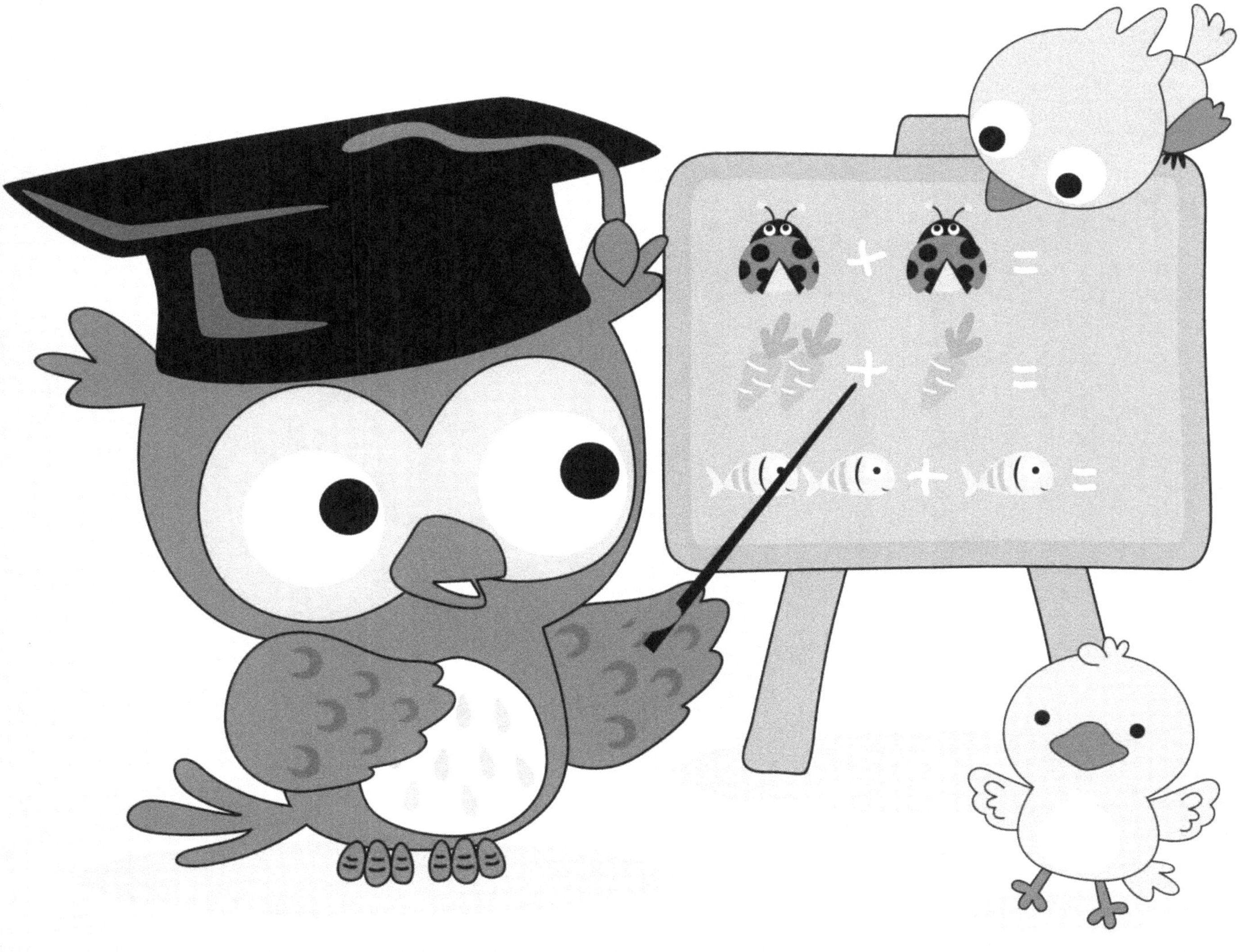

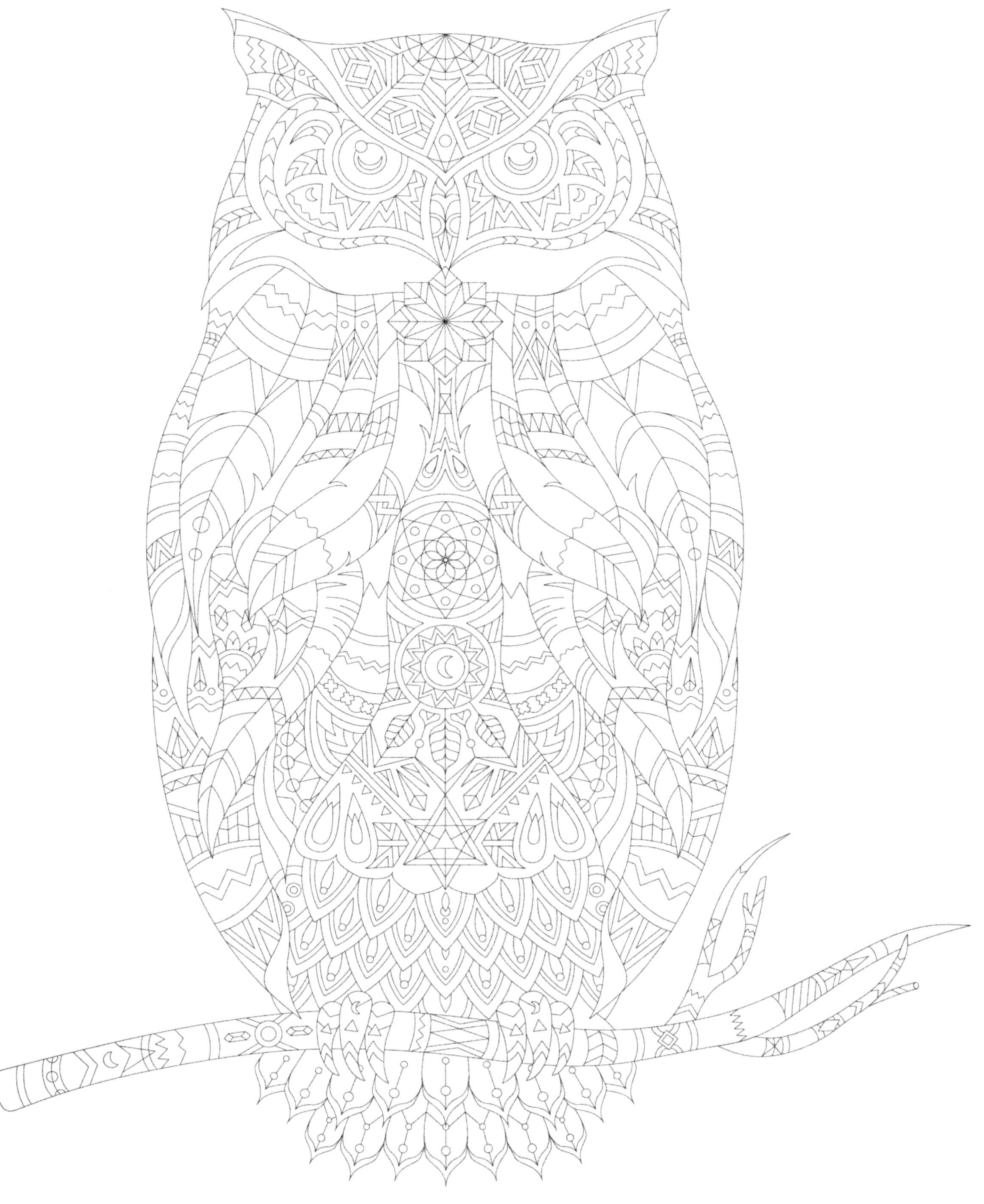

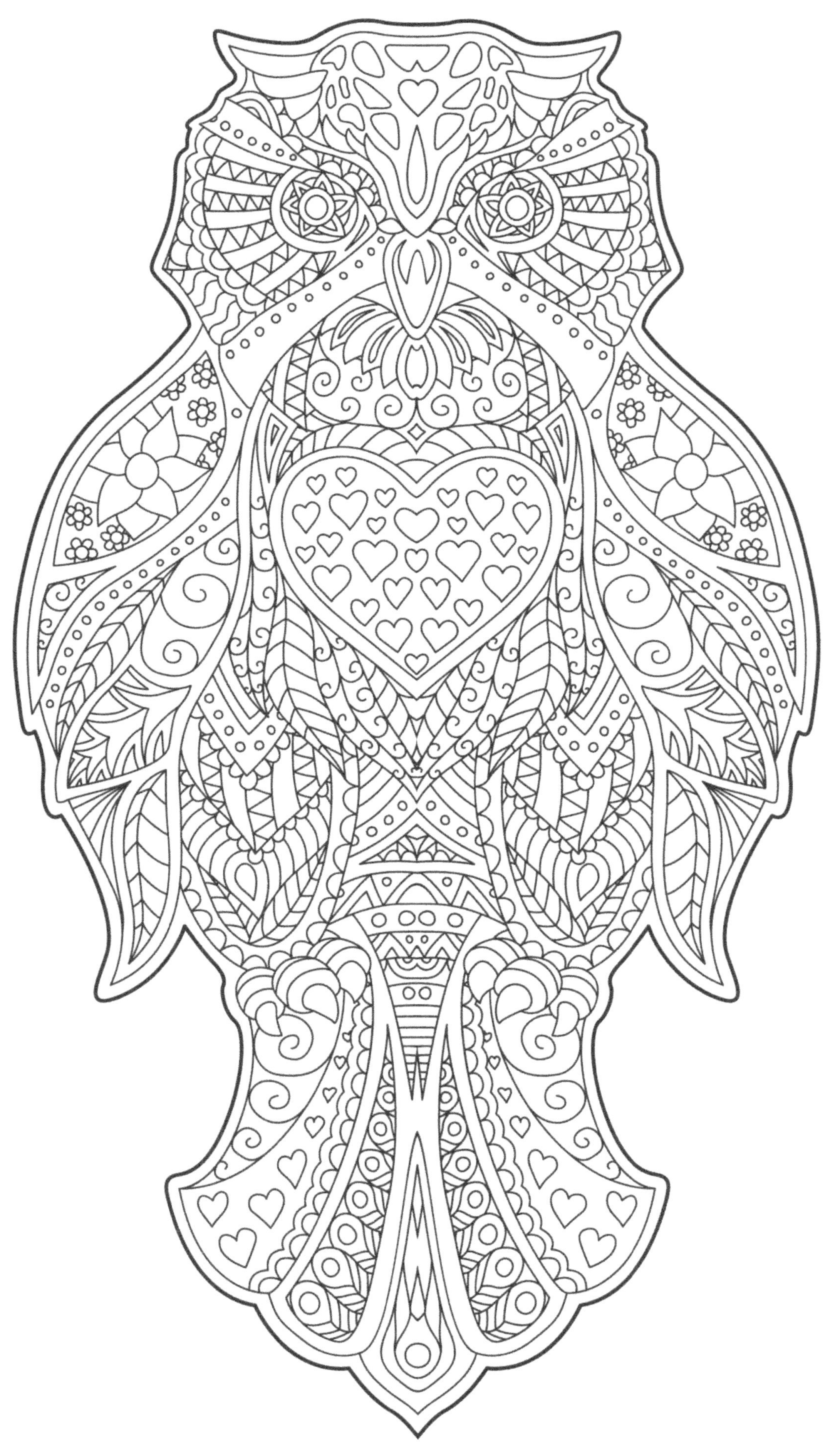

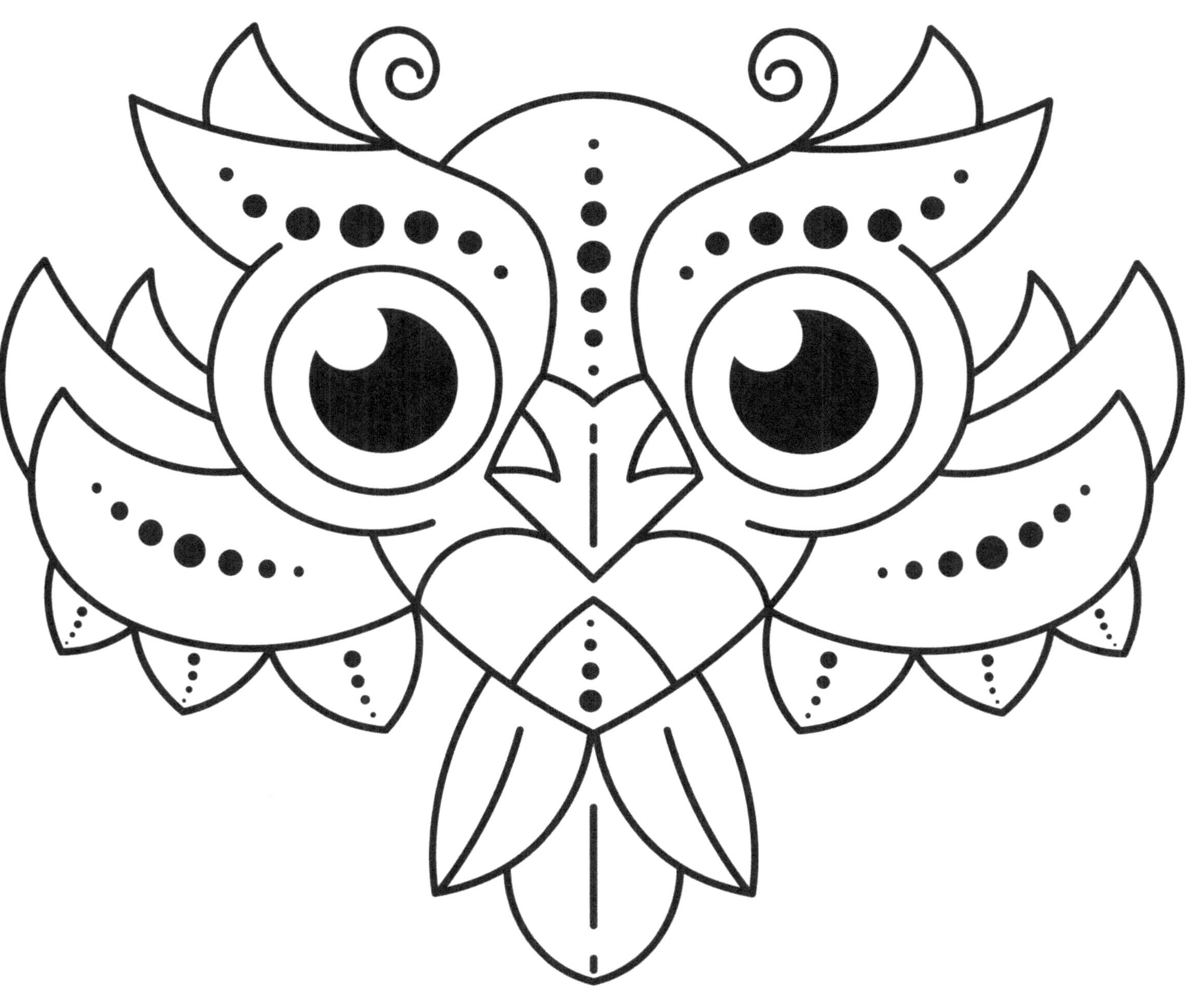

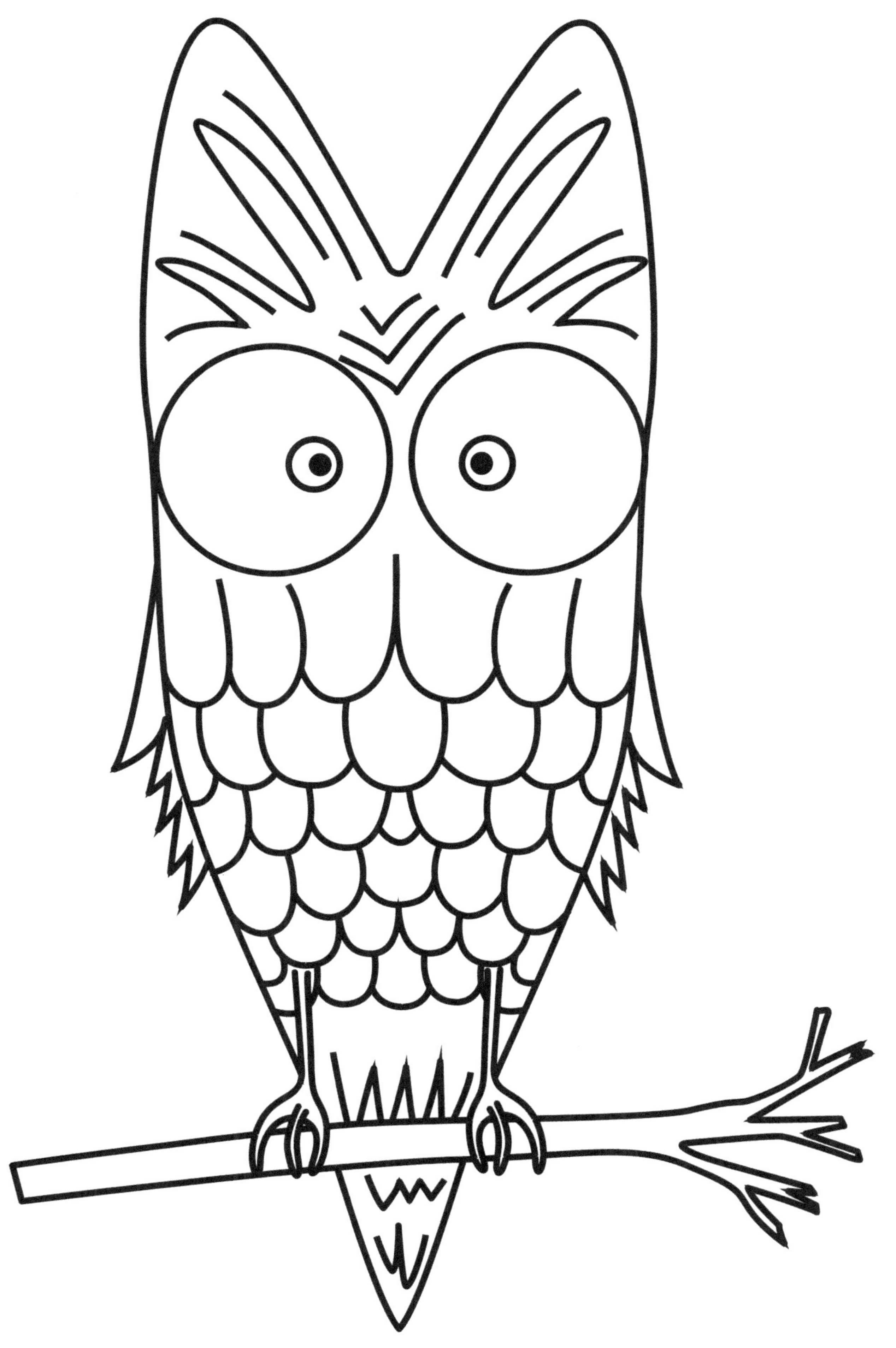

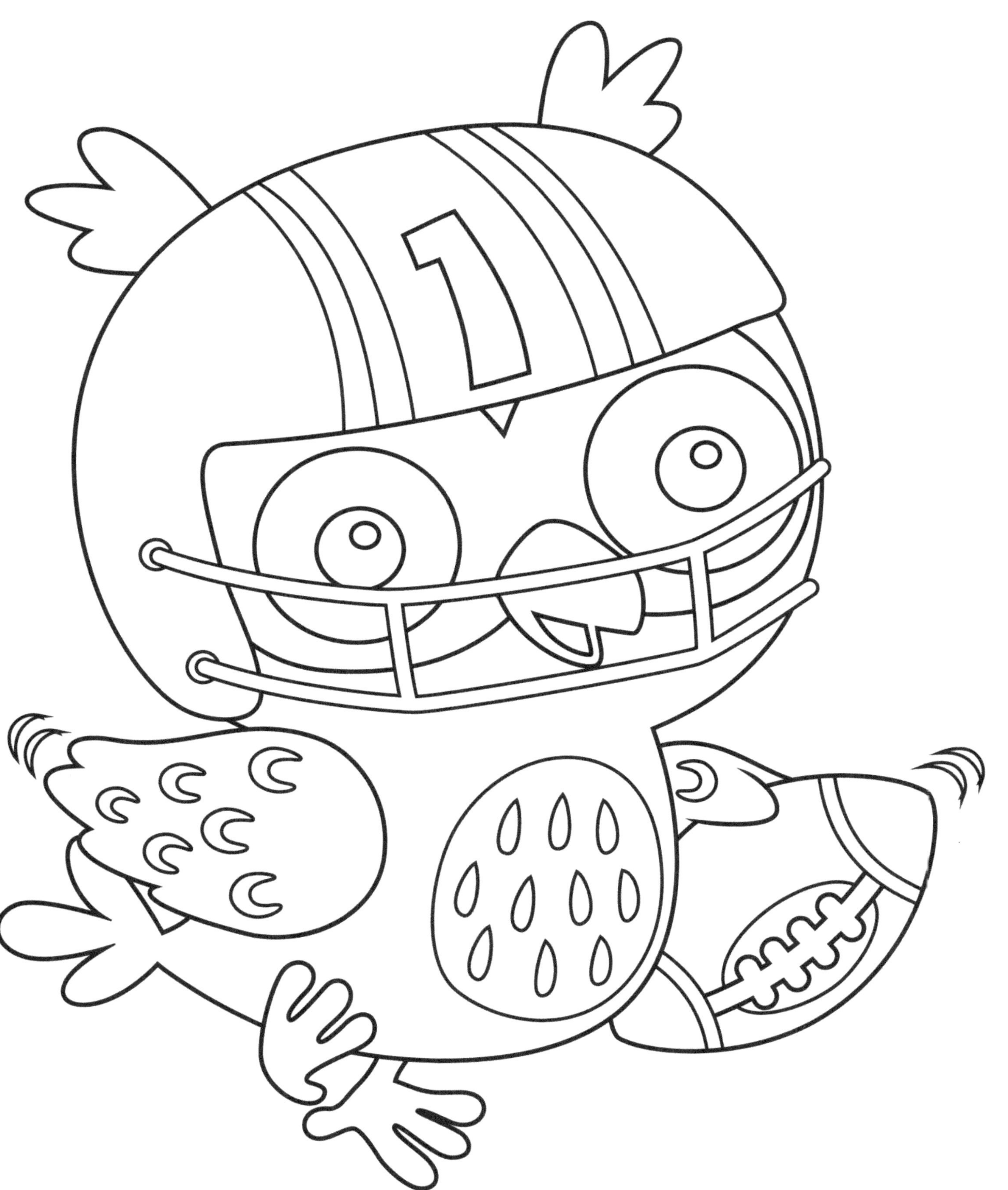

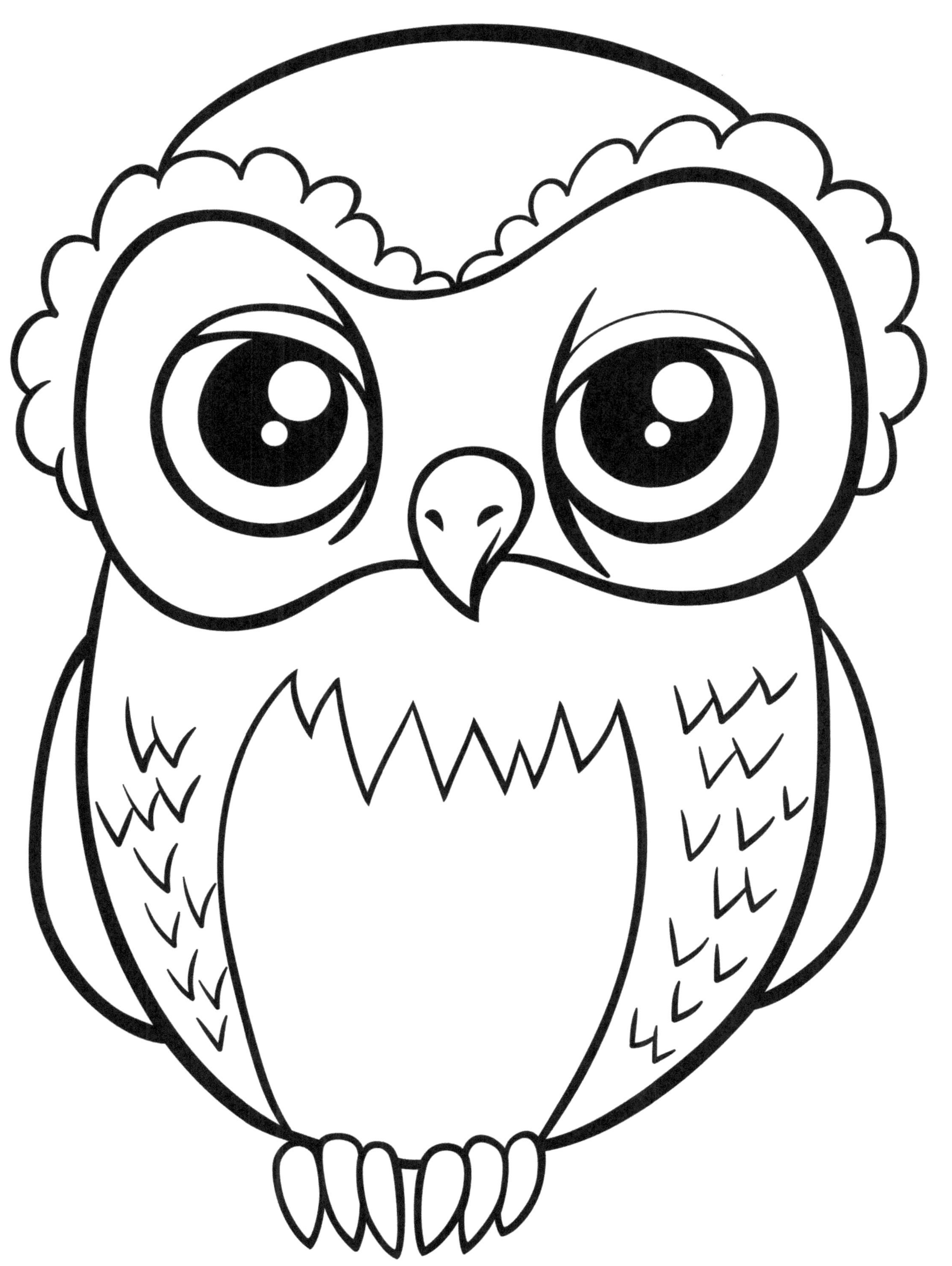

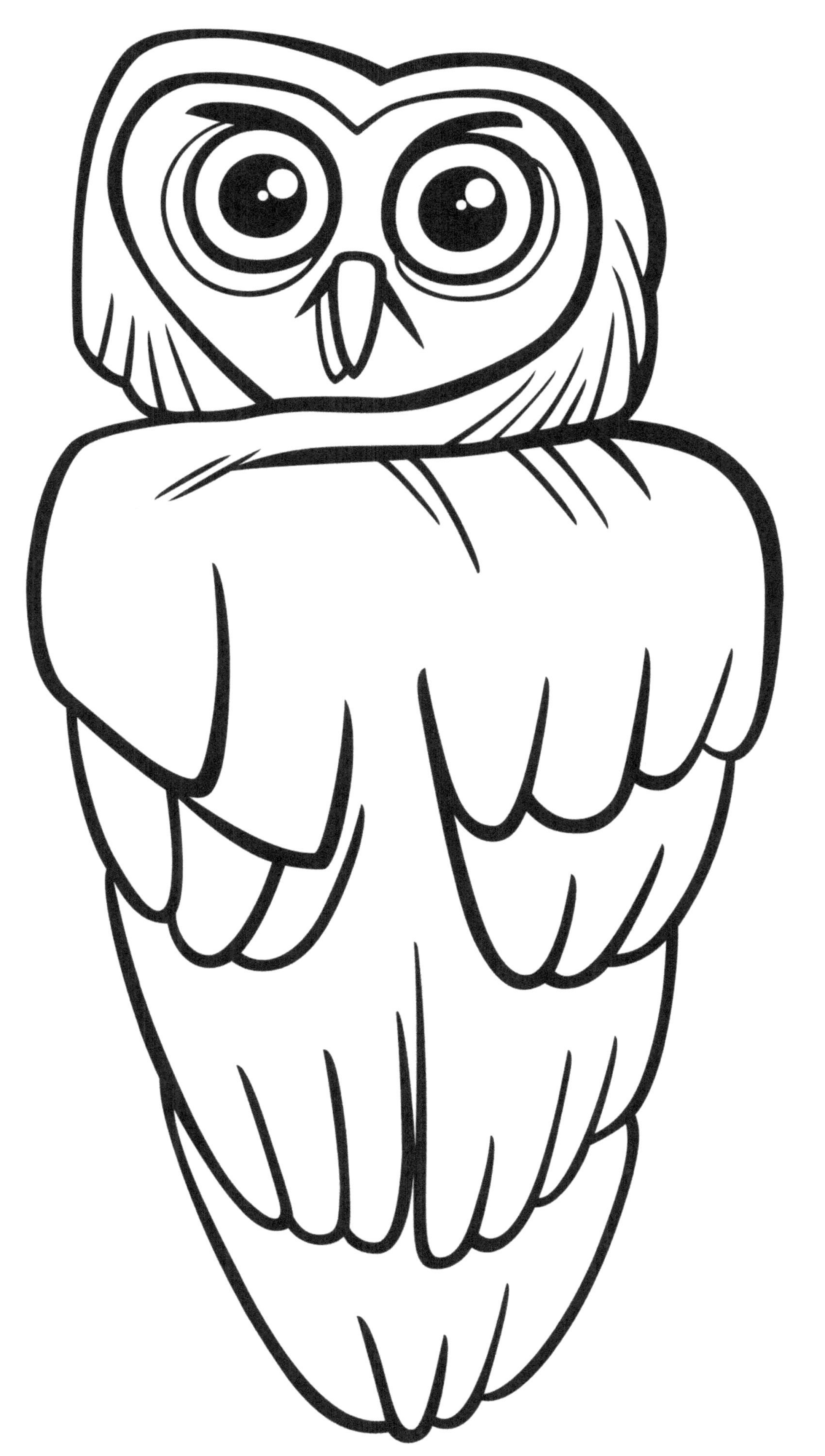

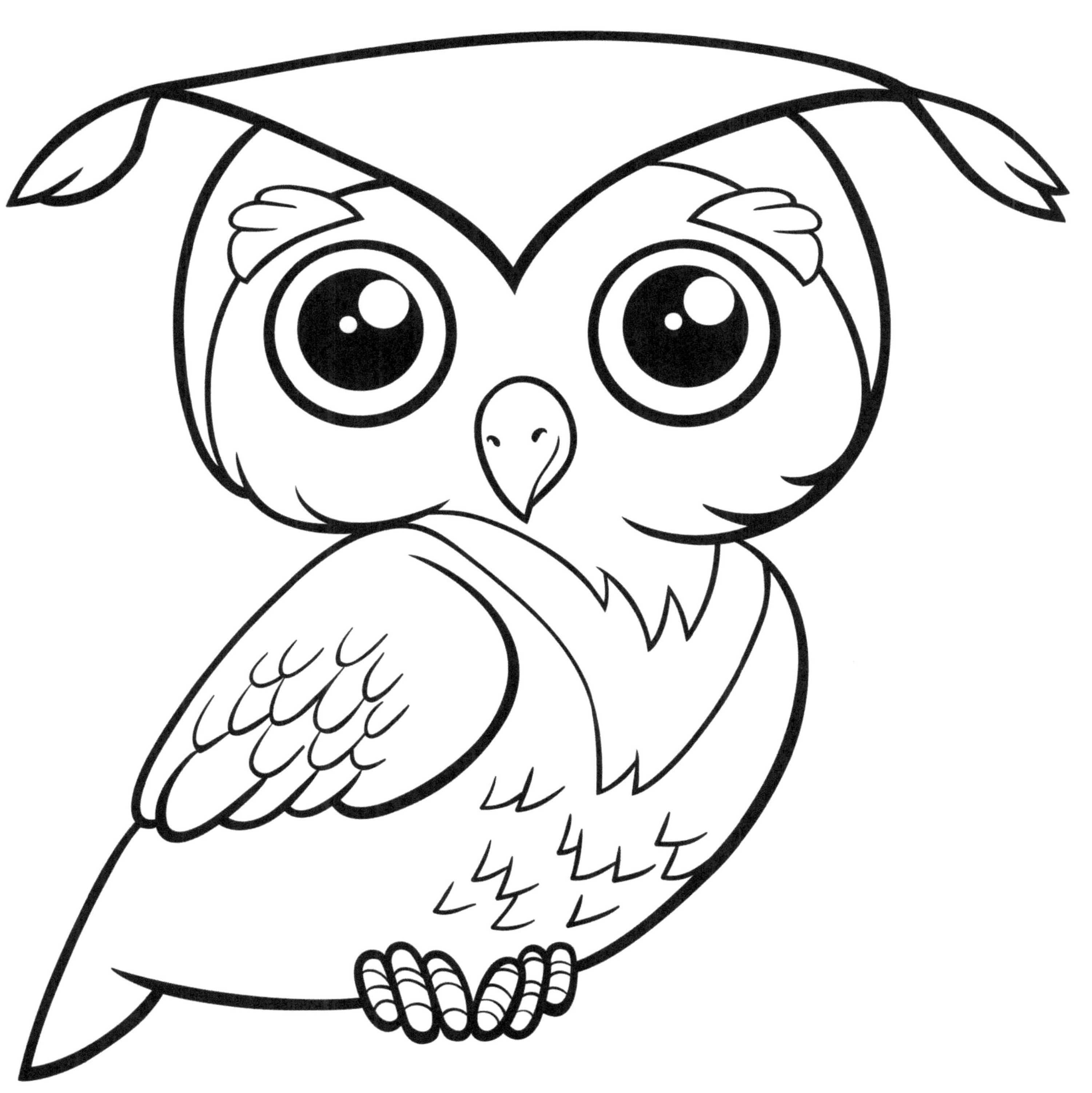

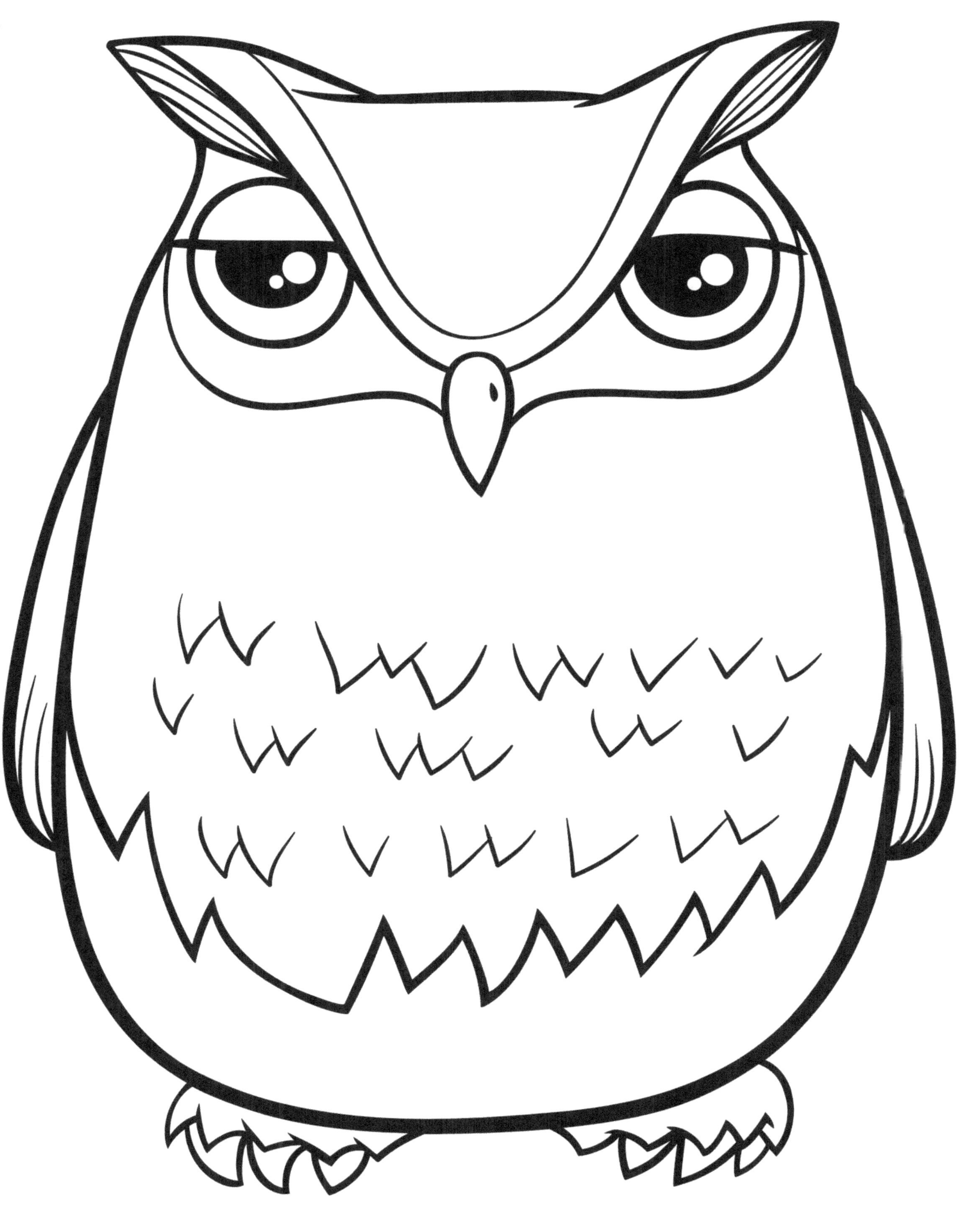

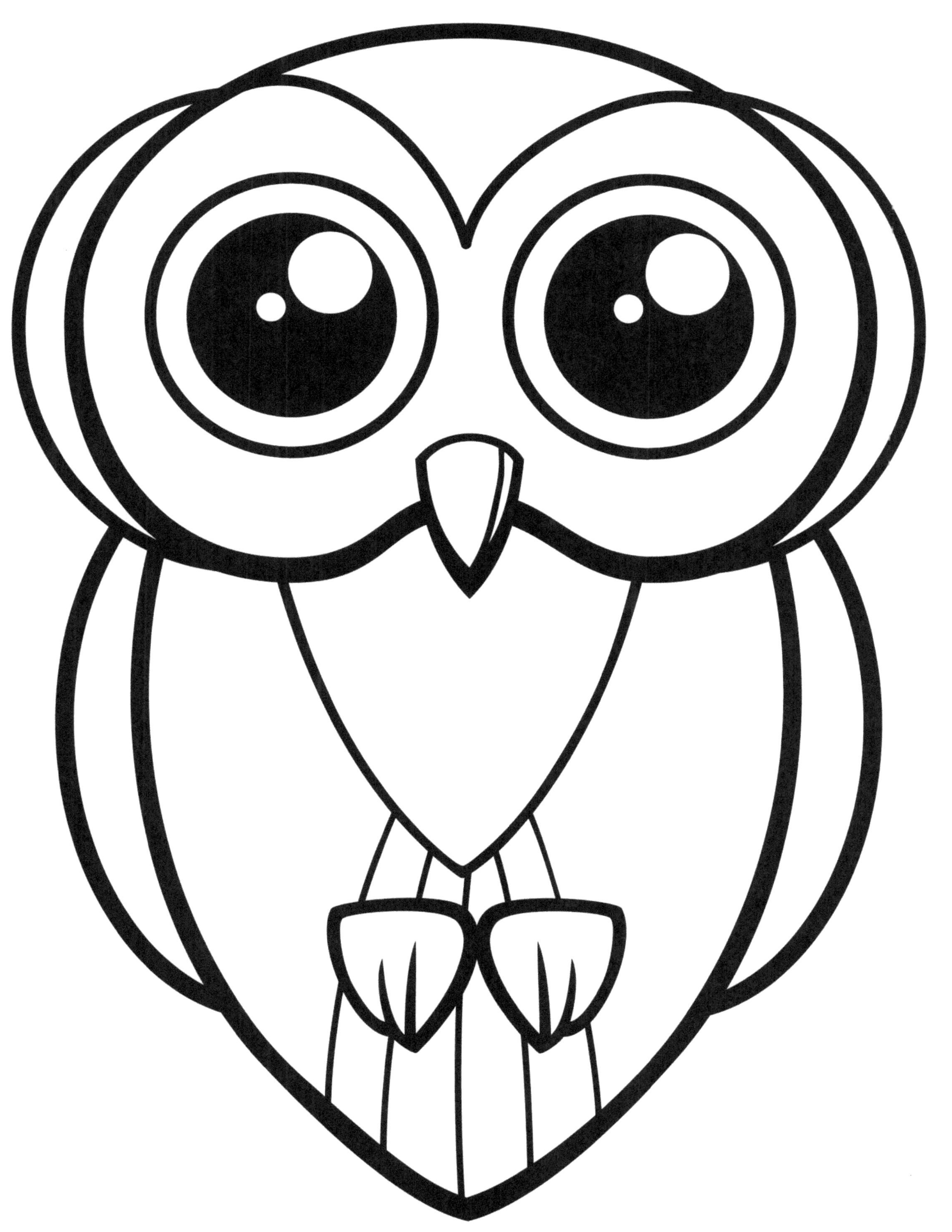

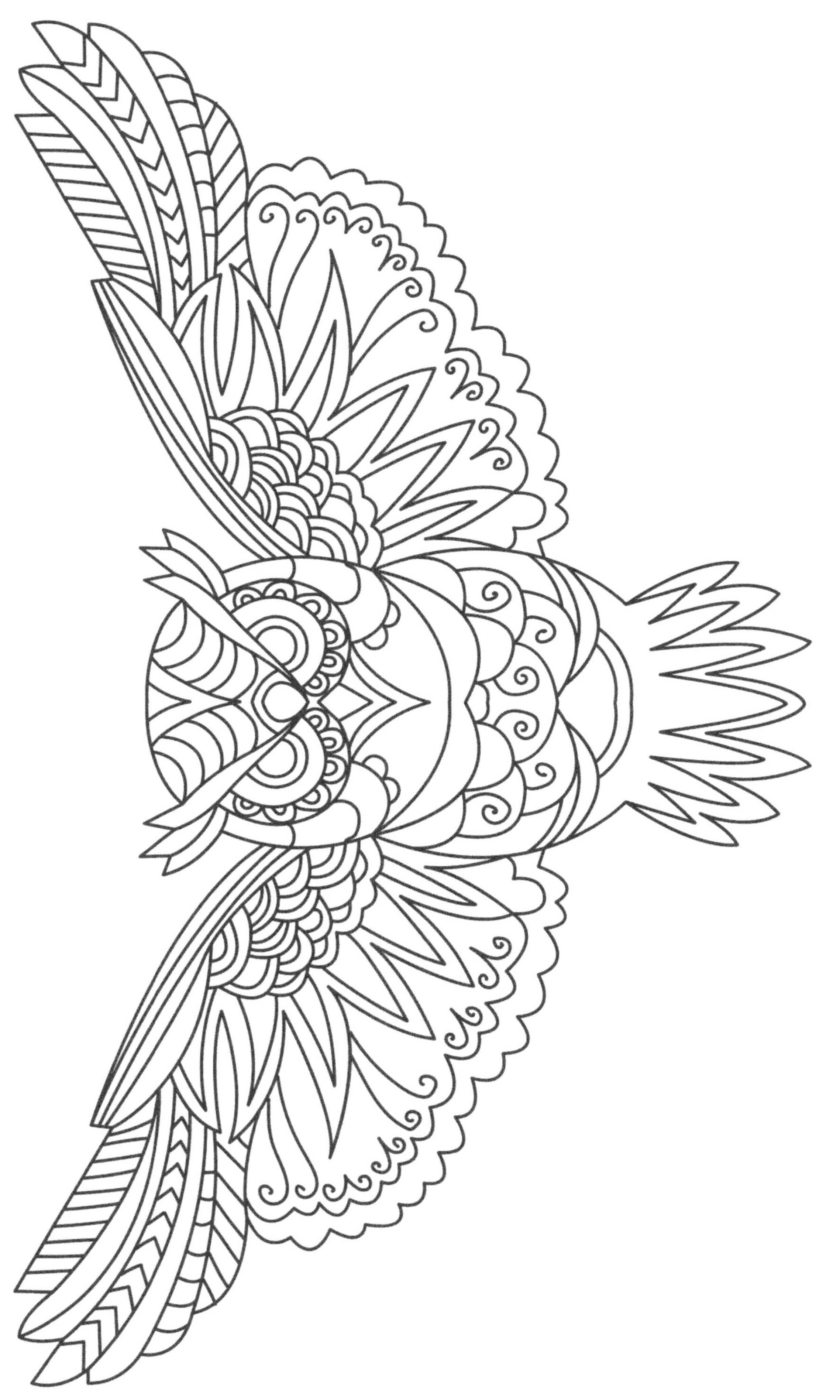

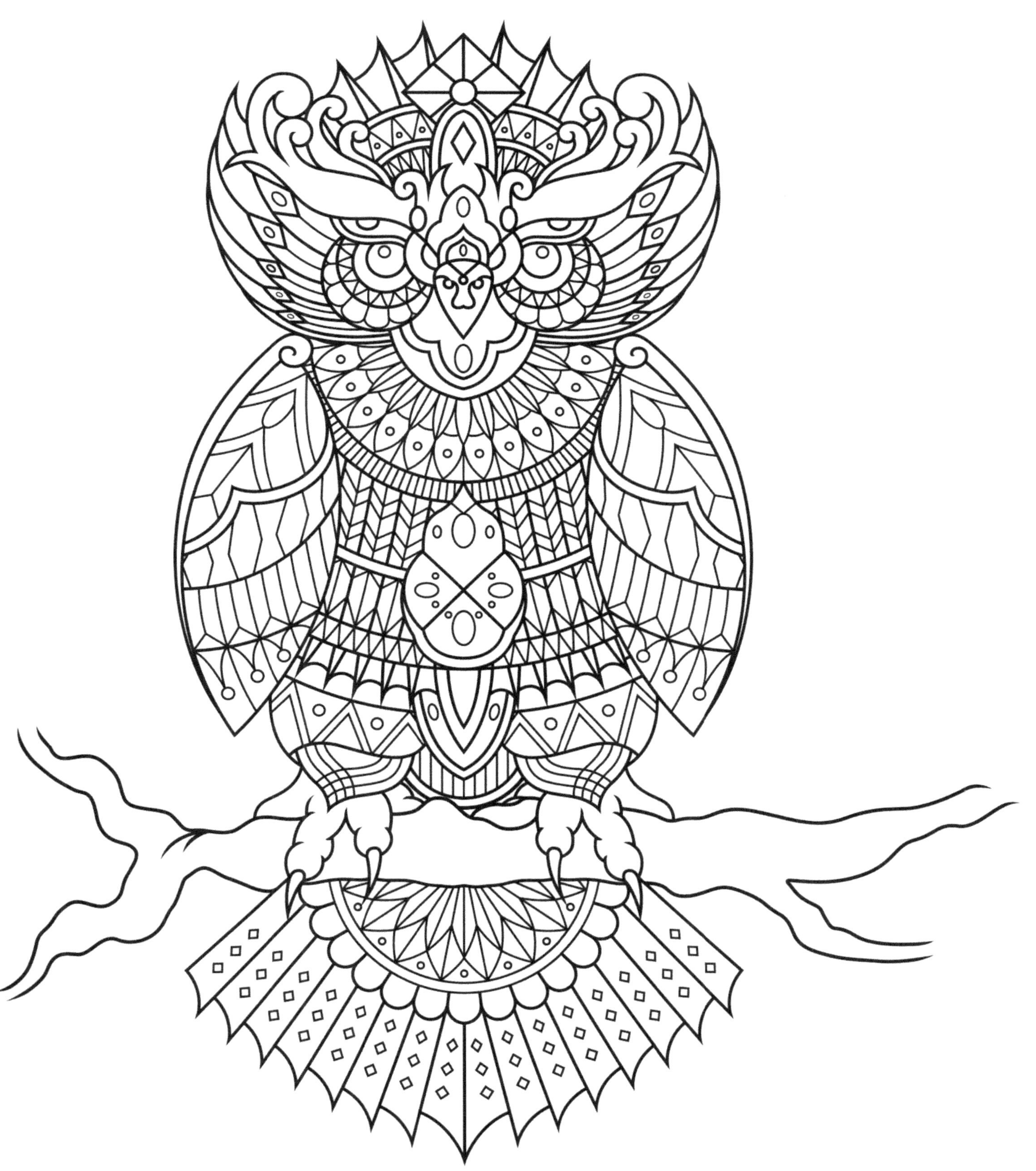

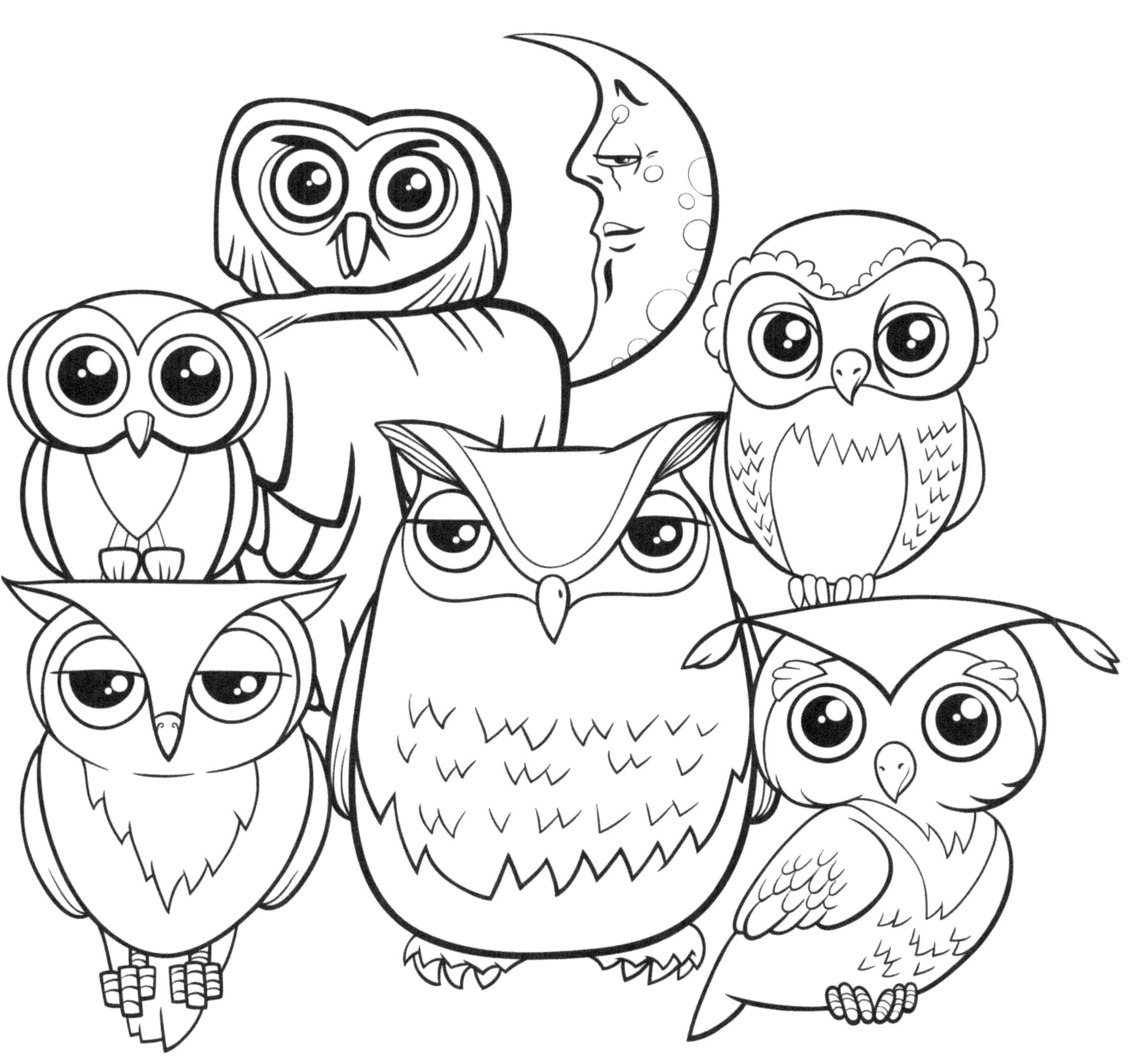

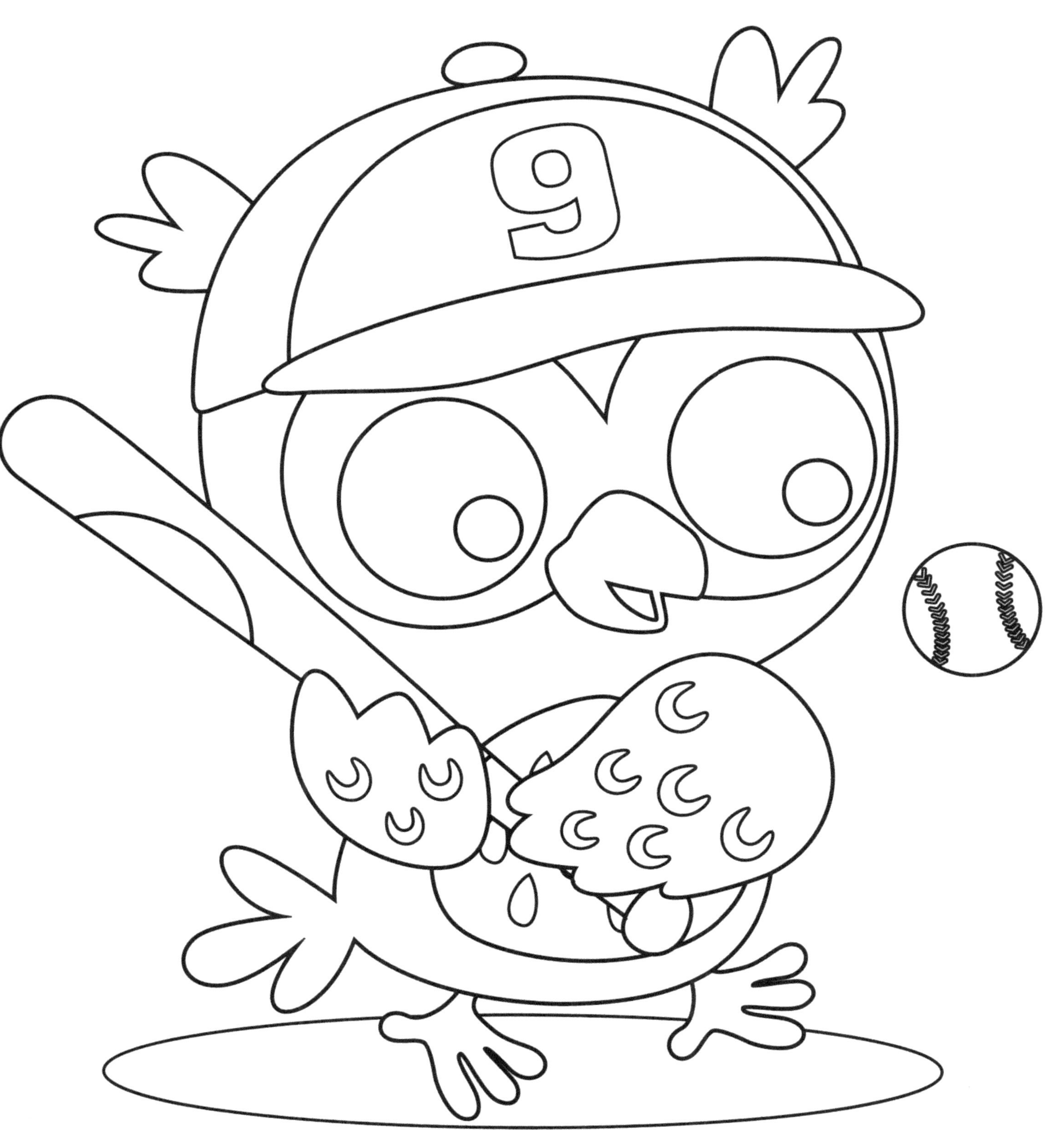

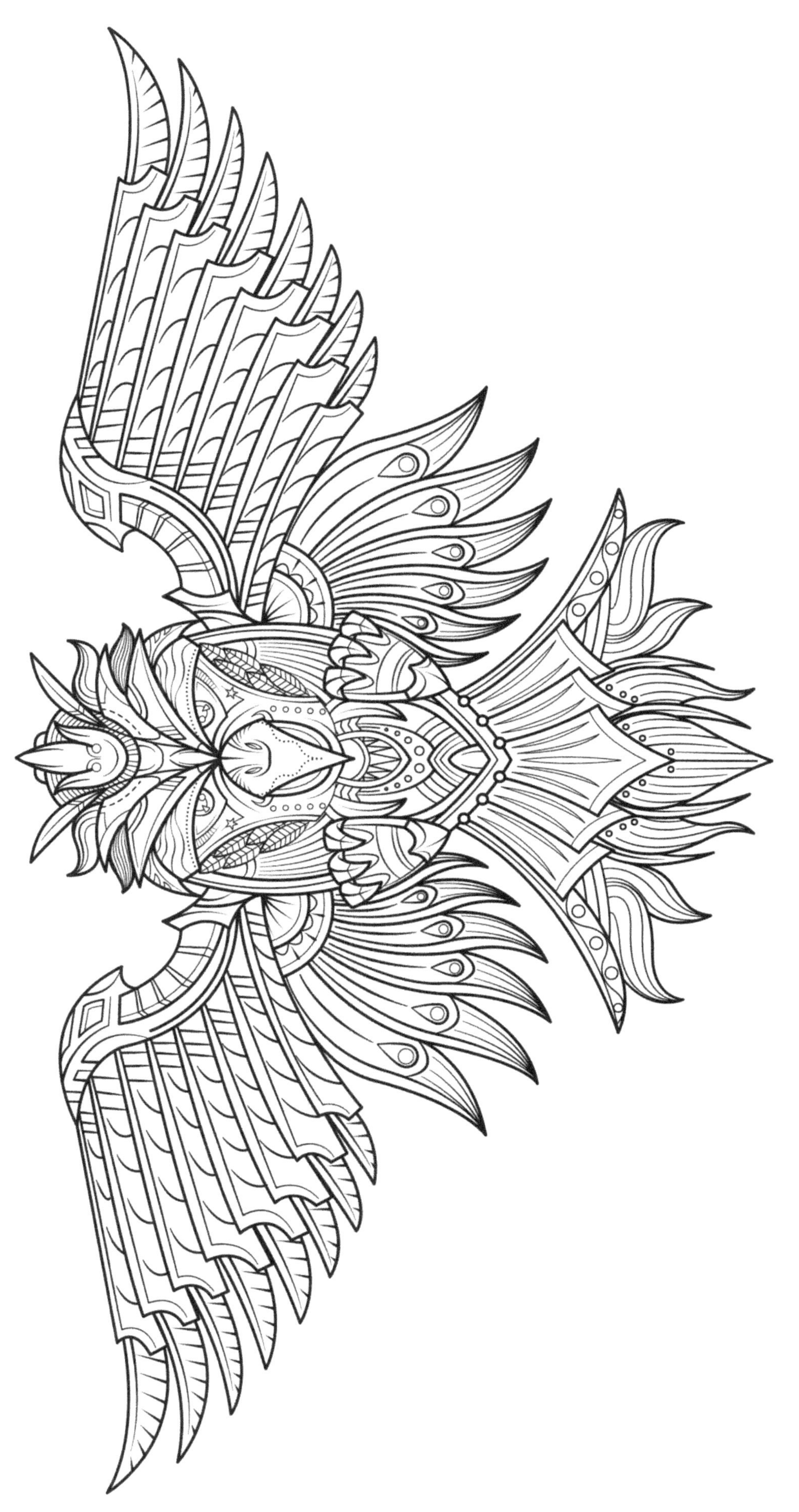

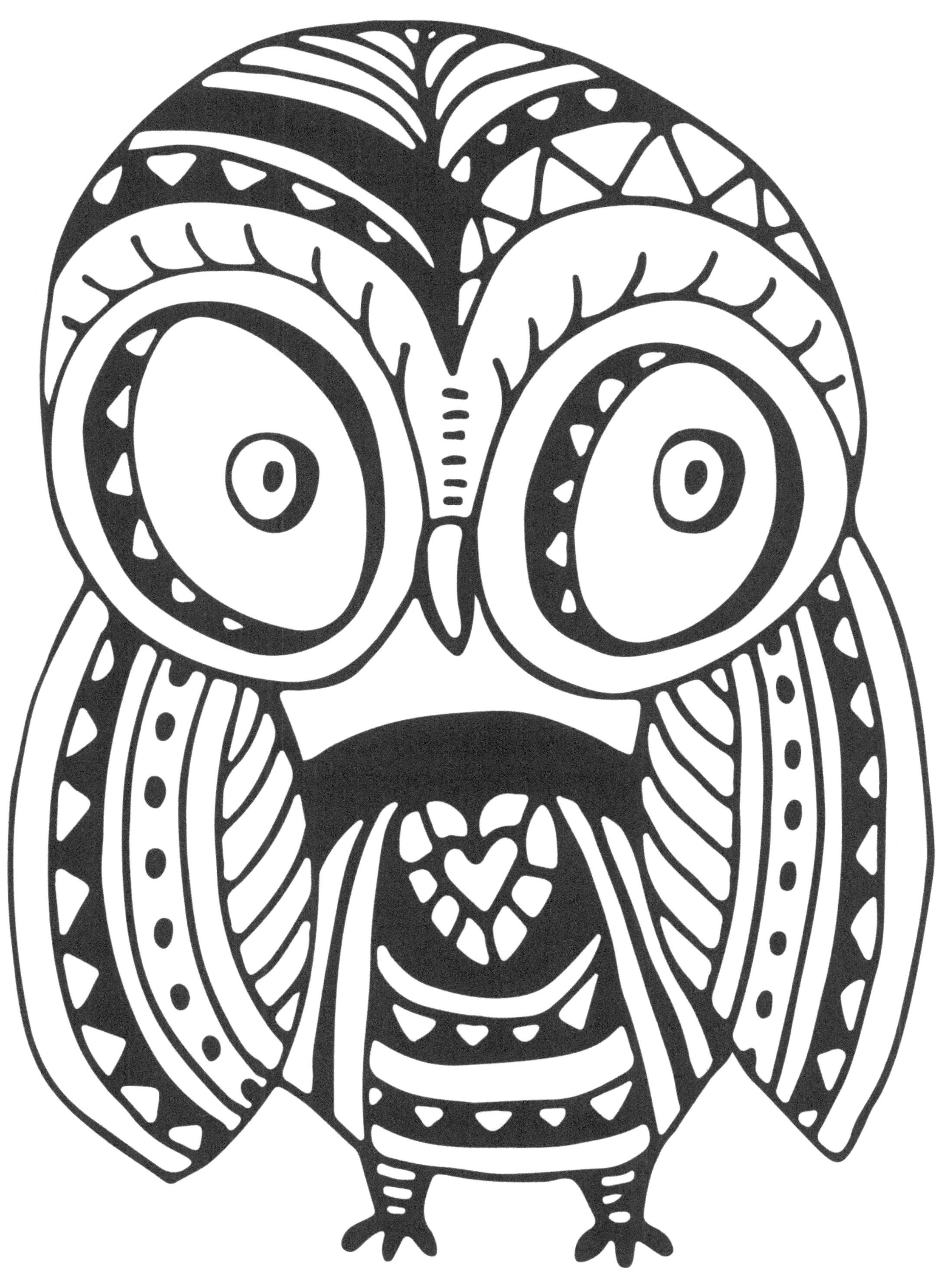

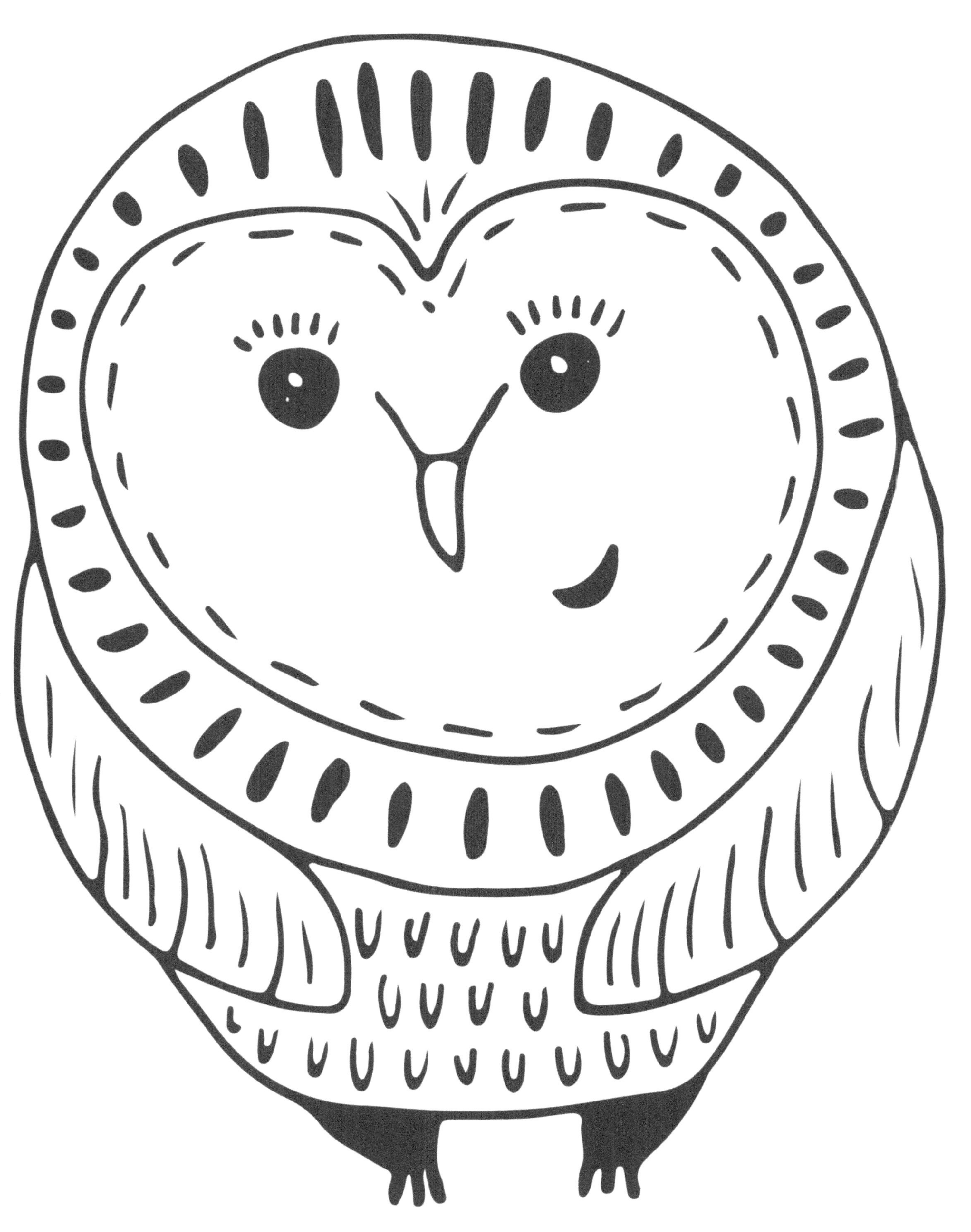

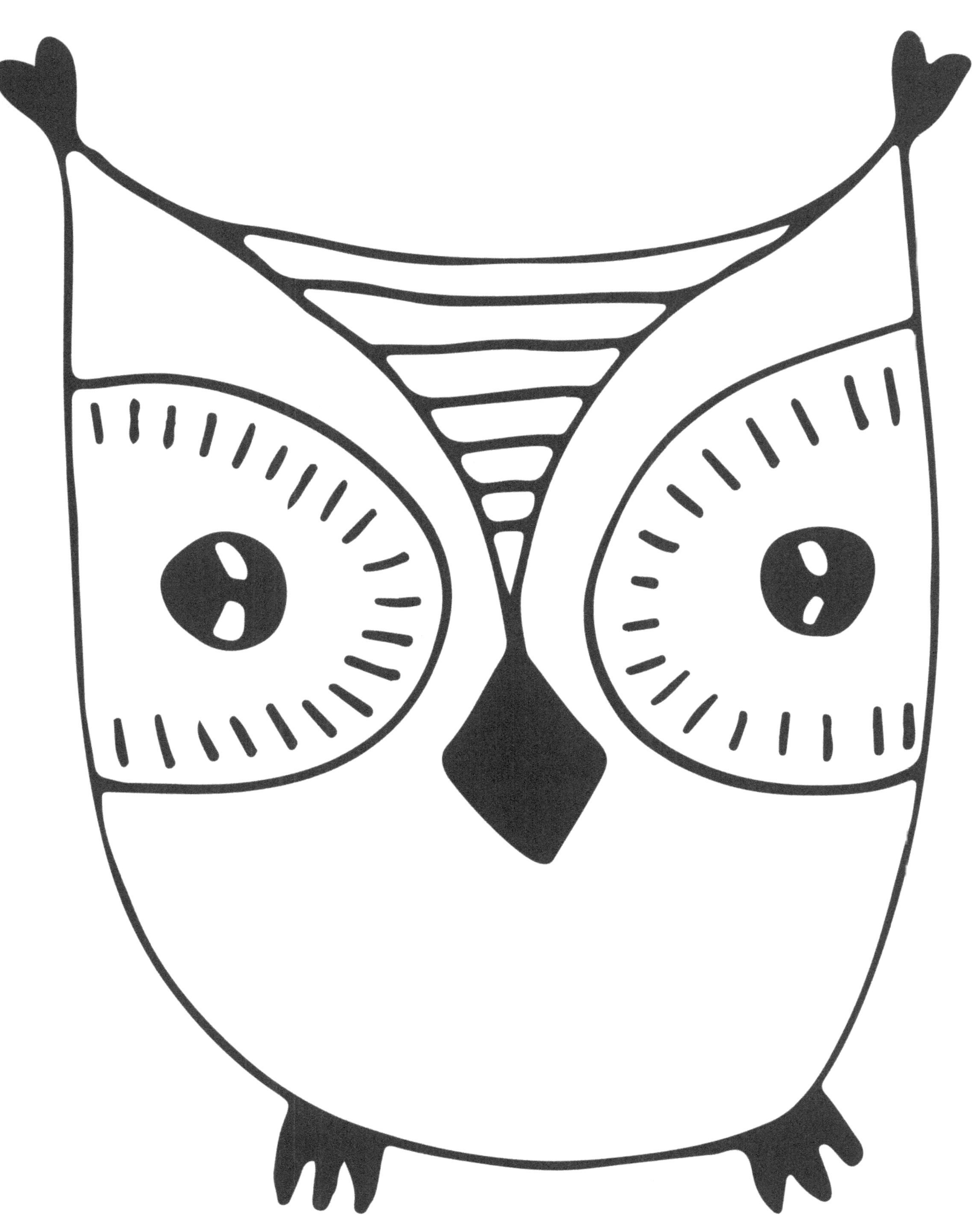

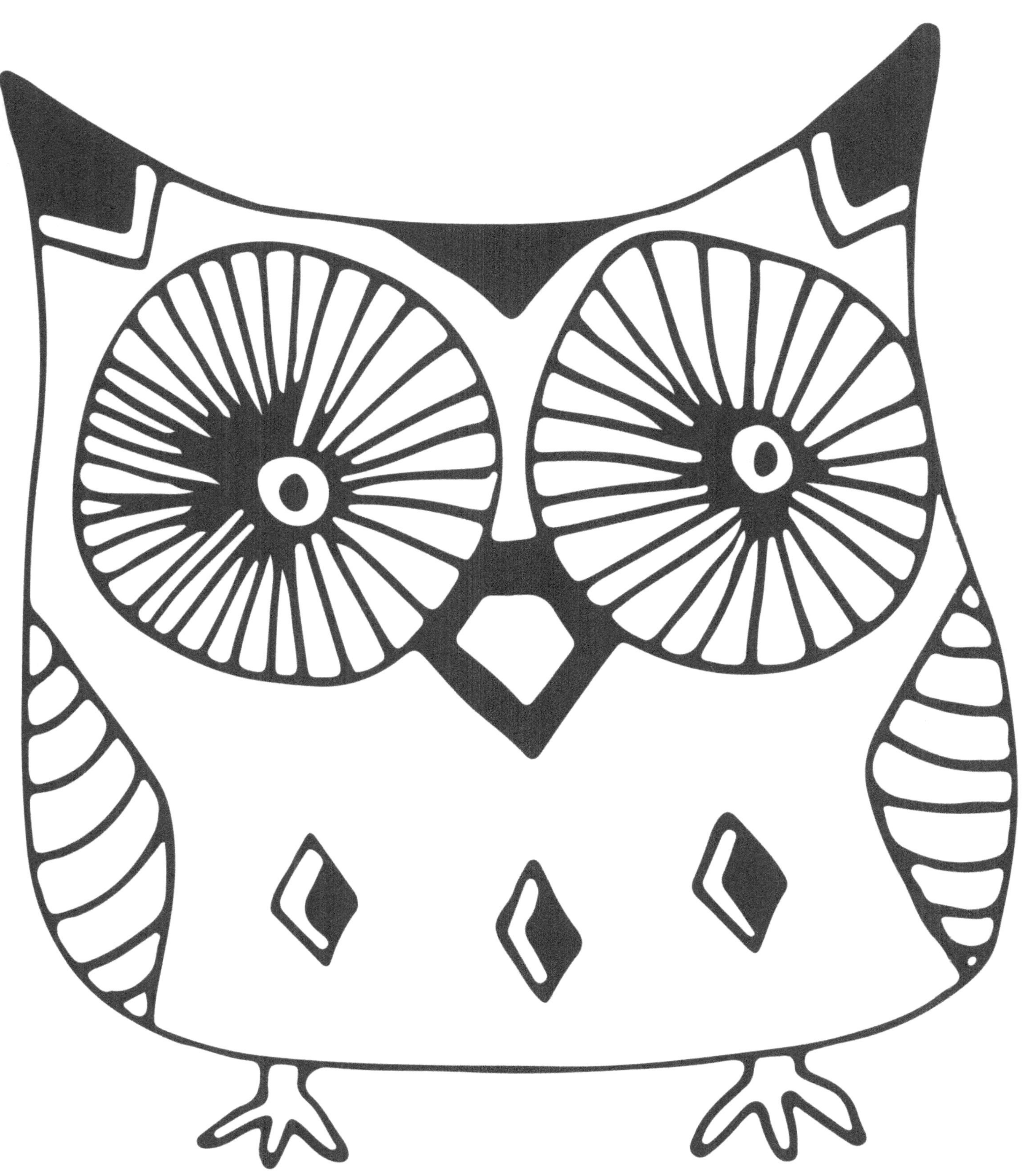

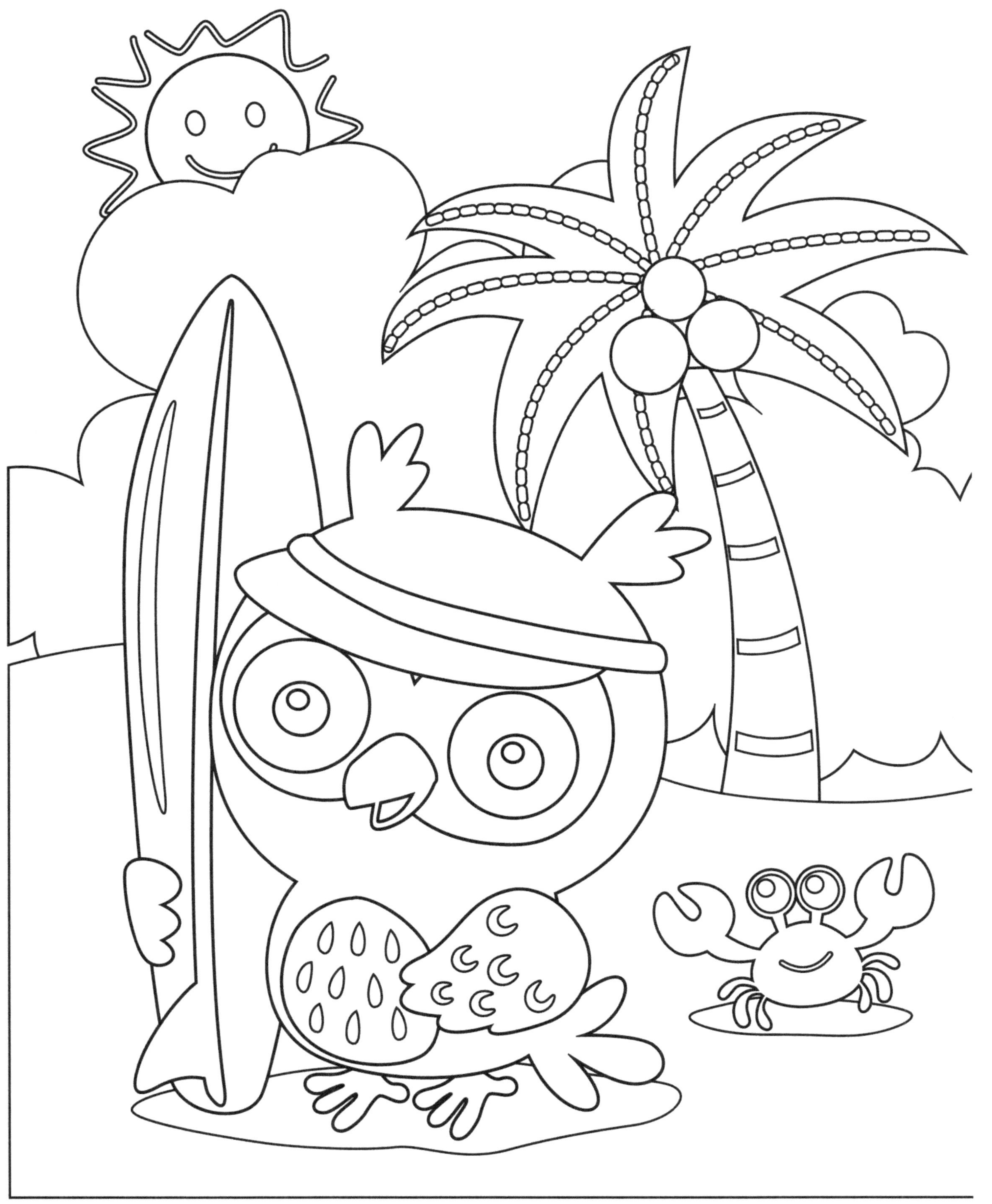

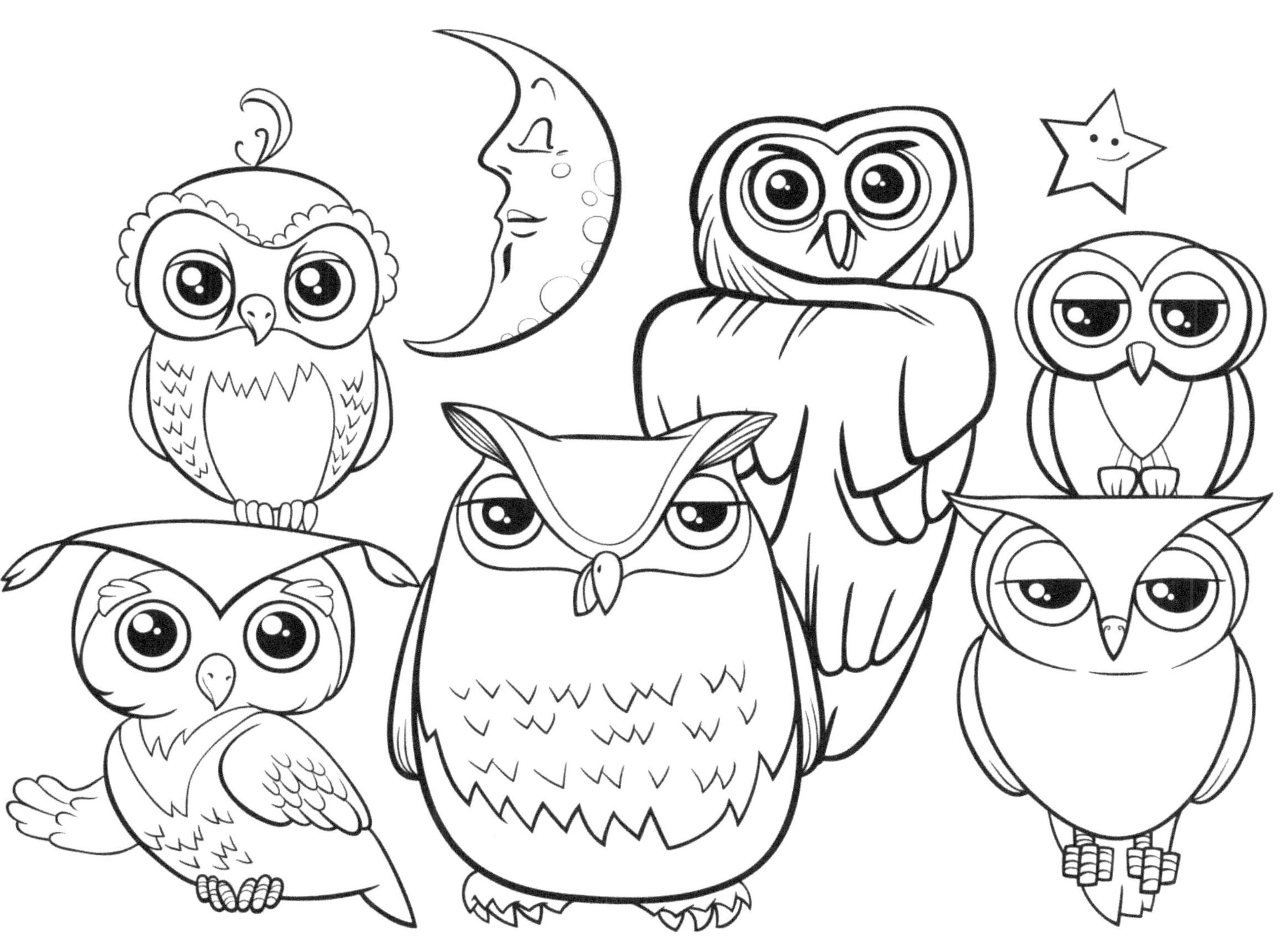

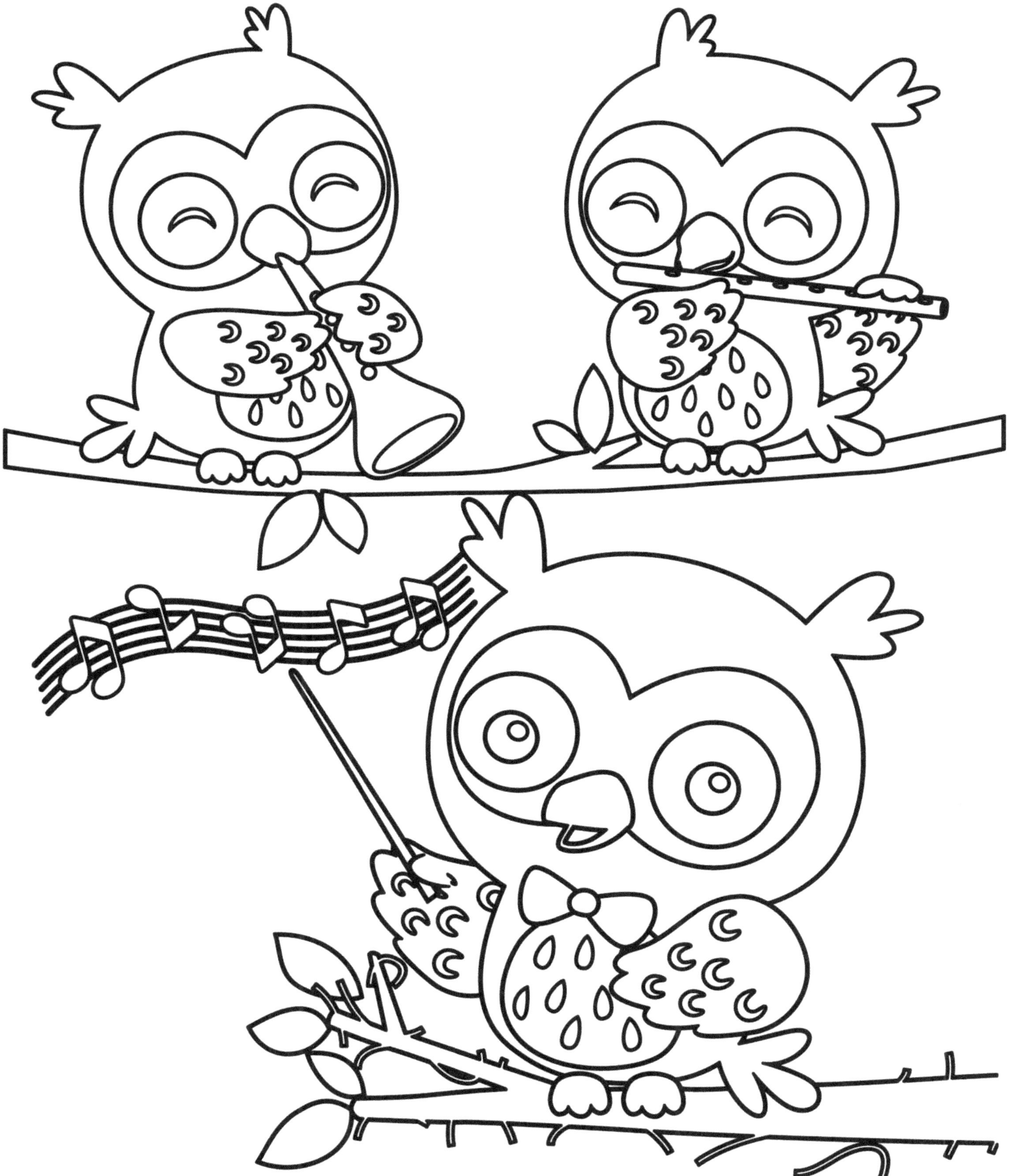

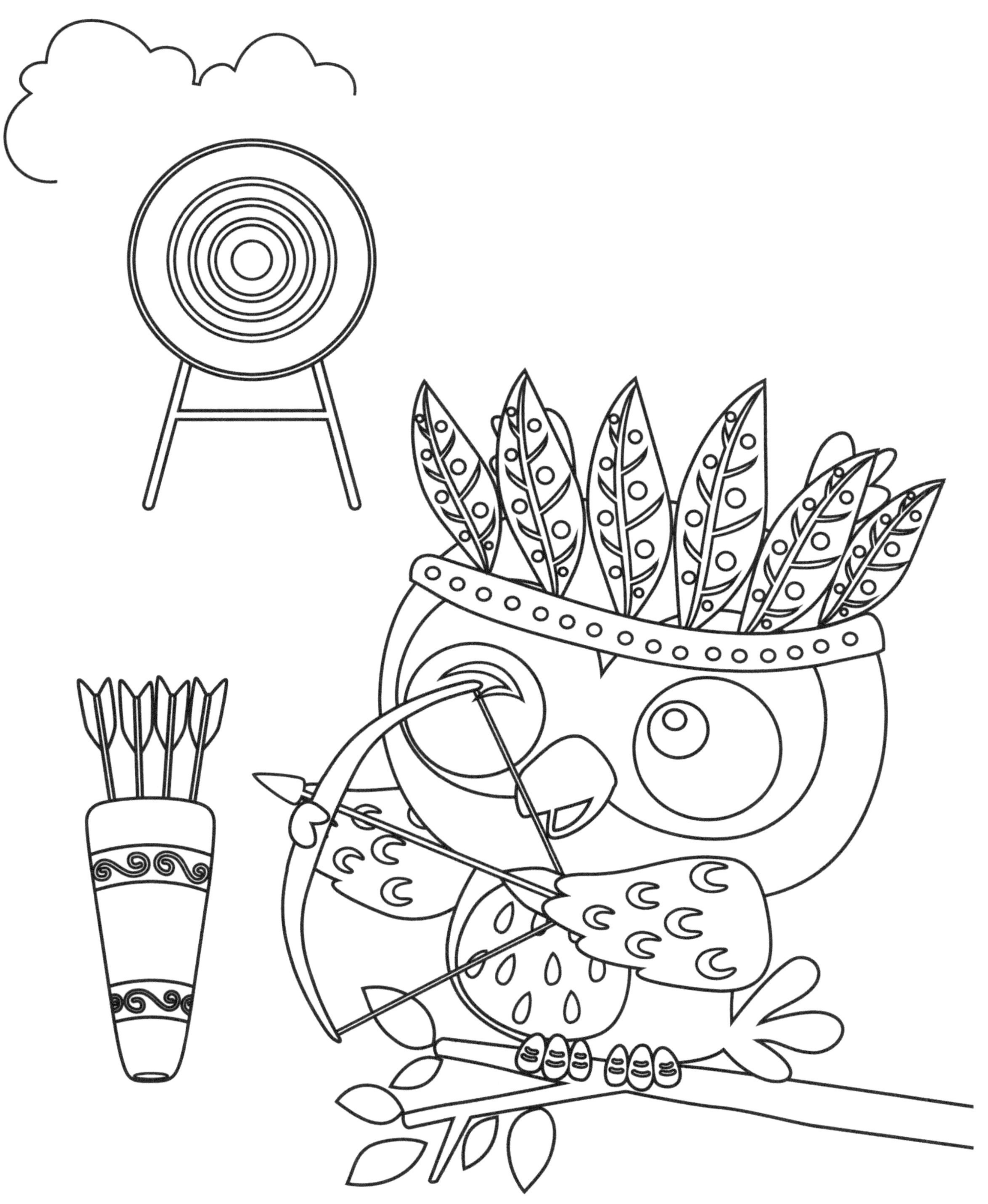

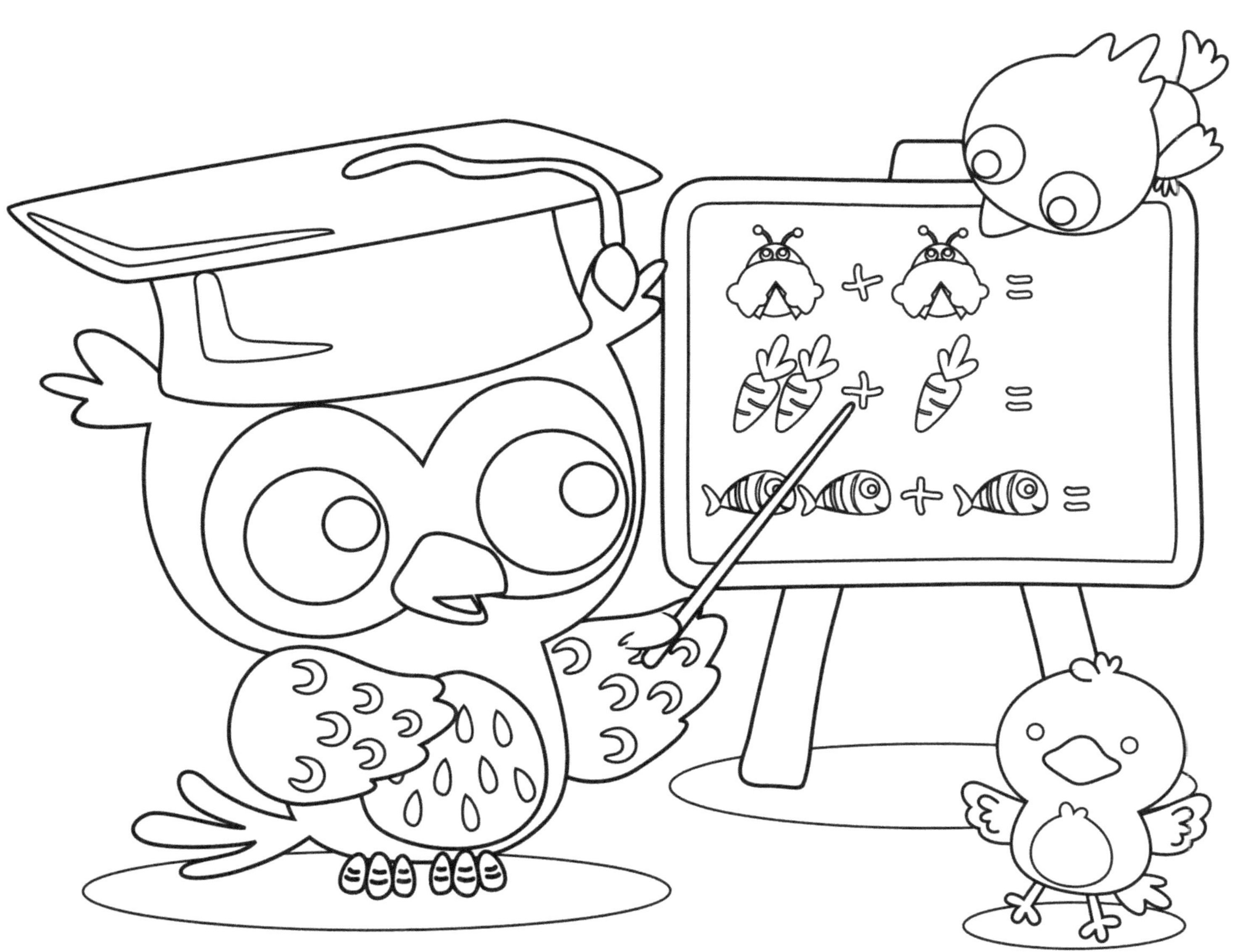